Microlife
That Makes Us Ill

Steve Parker

Chicago, Illinois

For information, address the publisher:
Raintree, 100 N. LaSalle, Suite 1200
Chicago, IL 60602
Customer Service 888-363-4266
Visit our website at www.raintreelibrary.com

Printed and bound in the United States
by Corporate Graphics
10 09
10 9 8 7 6 5 4 3 2

Edited by Katie Orchard
Designed by Tim Mayer
Picture Research by Lynda Lines and Frances Bailey
Production by Duncan Gilbert

Library of Congress Cataloging-in-Publication Data
Parker, Steve.
  Microlife that makes us ill / Steve Parker
    p. cm. -- (The amazing world of microlife)
  Includes bibliographical references and index.
  ISBN 1-4109-1847-5 (lib. bdg. : hardcover) --
  ISBN 1-4109-1852-1 (pbk.)
1. Pathogenic microorganisms--Juvenile literature.
2. Medical microbiology--Juvenile literature I. Title.
II. Series: Parker, Steve. Amazing world of microlife

QR175.P28 2005
616.9'041--dc22

2005004227

Acknowledgments
The publishers would like to thank the following for permission to reproduce photographs: Corbis p. **21** (Yann Arthus-Bertrand); Getty Images/Digital Vision p. **13**; photolibrary.com pp. **15** (Lise Metzger), **27** (Mike Birkhead); Rex Features p. **5** top (SIPA); Science Photo Library pp. **1** (VVG), **3** (Biophoto Associates), **4** (Dr. Linda Stannard, UCT), **5** bottom (David Scharf), **6** (Alfred Pasieka), **8** (BSIP VEM), **9** (Mark Clarke), **10** (S. J. Krasemann), **11** (Andrew Syred), **12** (Dr. Gopal Murti), **14** (Eye of Science), **16** (Mona Lisa Production), **17** (Michael Donne), **19** (VVG), **20** (Biophoto Associates), **22** (Gerald C. Kelly), **23** (Eye of Science), **24** (Sinclair Stammers), **25** (R. Umesh Chandran/TDR/WHO), **26** (CNRI), **28**; Still Pictures p. **18** (Hartmut Schwarzbach); Topfoto pp. **7** (Steven Rubin/The Image Works), **29** (Bob Daemmrich/The Image Works).

Cover photograph of a blood-sucking human body louse reproduced with permission of Science Photo Library (David Scharf).

Every effort has been made to contact copyright holders of any material reproduced in this book. Any omissions will be rectified in subsequent printings if notice is given to the publishers.

The paper used to print this book comes from sustainable resources.

Contents

Some words are shown in bold, **like this**. You can find out what they mean by looking in the Glossary.

Microlife Is Everywhere!

Look at the air around you. What do you see? Aside from a few bits of floating dust, not much. Air seems clear and clean. What about the things in your home, such as the tables and chairs, or even this book? They probably seem clean, too.

The "hidden world"

If you could look much closer, you would see little living things all around. Some are smaller than specks of dust. If you could peer even closer, you would see even tinier living things. Our own eyes cannot do this. We need to use powerful magnifying glasses, and even more powerful **microscopes**, to reveal this "hidden world" of microlife.

Viruses are the smallest microlife. These viruses cause common colds, making us sniffle and sneeze.

From the moment we are born, our bodies learn to fight and destroy harmful microlife.

War on germs

Some microlife is harmless, but some is not. Bugs and germs are always trying to attack us. There are some things we can do to fight back and defeat them. You can read about them in this book.

strand of cloth

bacteria

A microscope shows bloblike microlife called **bacteria**. These ones are on the strands of a dishcloth.

The Smallest Bugs

The smallest of all living things are germs called **viruses**. They come in many different shapes, such as rods, balls, and boxes. Viruses get into the body in a lot of different ways. They can get into us on food, in drink, through skin cuts, or in air. Different kinds of viruses cause colds, flu (influenza), **chickenpox**, and small lumps called warts on the skin.

This virus is called *morbilli*. It causes measles, when many itchy spots appear on the skin.

HOW BIG ARE VIRUSES? Viruses are so small that a pile of 1 million would just fit on the period at the end of this sentence.

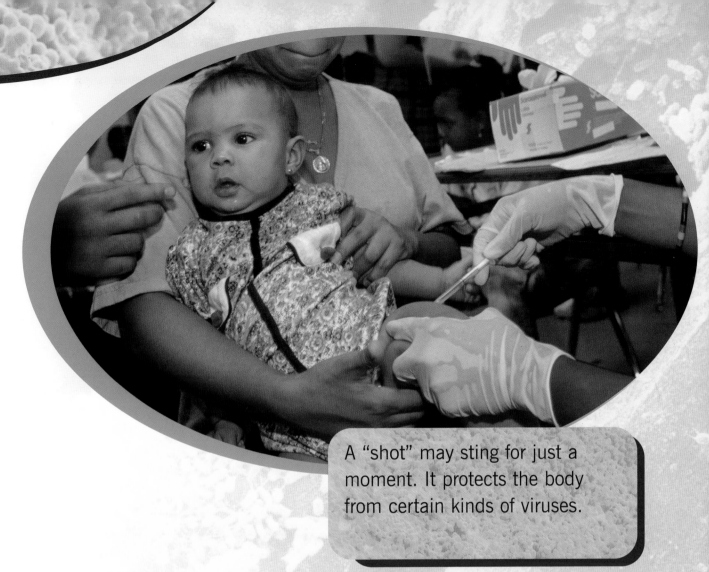

A "shot" may sting for just a moment. It protects the body from certain kinds of viruses.

Fighting viruses

If we have an illness caused by a virus, we should stay warm and rest. We should sneeze or cough into a tissue. Otherwise we spray millions of viruses into the air, which other people may catch. We can beat viruses with "shots" (**vaccinations**). A "shot" puts a substance into the body that helps it to fight against illnesses such as **measles**, **mumps**, and **rubella**.

Second-Smallest Bugs

The second-smallest germs, after **viruses**, are **bacteria**. Imagine that you could shrink a sports stadium so that it would fit into this "o." Then the people inside would be as tiny as bacteria.

What bacteria do

Bacteria get into the body in many ways. Some are breathed in, while others get in through a skin cut or in bad food and dirty water. Different kinds of bacteria cause different illnesses. Some cause a skin boil (painful red spot) or a sore throat. Others cause serious diseases such as blood poisoning.

Bacteria come in lots of different shapes. These ball-shaped bacteria are called *Streptococcus*.

Fighting bacteria

We can battle against bacteria and other germs by keeping ourselves, our clothes, and our homes clean. We should wash cuts and grazes carefully, and make sure they are covered. Many bacteria can be killed by medicine called **antibiotics**.

Many bacteria live in soil and dirt, so cuts and scrapes should be cleaned carefully.

KILLING BACTERIA

People use special substances called **antiseptics** to clean dirty cuts and kill bacteria on the body. They use **disinfectants** to kill germs in kitchens and bathrooms.

Flies, Food, and Germs

Flies and similar creatures carry microlife on their bodies. If a fly lands on our food, and then we eat it, the microlife gets into us. Flies also land on kitchen objects, such as worktops, plates, and cups. We keep all these things clean, and wash our hands often.

One housefly can carry 1 million bacteria and other germs.

Microlife inside us

Some kinds of tiny **bacteria** live inside us all the time, in our intestines (guts). Usually these bacteria are friendly, such as the *E. coli* bacteria. They help our bodies to get **nutrients** from food.

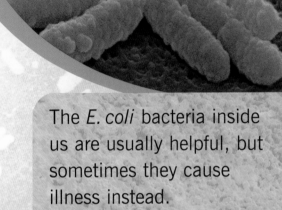

The *E. coli* bacteria inside us are usually helpful, but sometimes they cause illness instead.

Sometimes these bacteria become harmful. This may happen if we do not eat enough healthy foods. Then we feel sick. We need to rest and drink plenty of water. If we become really sick, we may need medicine from the doctor.

FRIENDLY BACTERIA
The billions of friendly bacteria inside our bodies would fill about three coffee cups.

Micropests

Microlife loves warm, damp places—especially the kinds of microlife called **protists**. These are tiny, Jell-O-like creatures. They are bigger than **bacteria**, but still too small for us to see without a **microscope**. One terrible disease caused by protists is **malaria**. It causes great fever, shaking, and vomiting, and is spread by insects called mosquitoes.

healthy blood cell

protist inside blood cell

TERRIBLE TOLL
Every minute in the world, about five people die of malaria. Many are young children.

Malaria is caused by plasmodium protists, which have infected these blood cells.

Dangerous bites

Mosquitoes feed on blood. If a mosquito bites a person with malaria, the mosquito sucks in some malaria protists. The mosquito may then pass on a tiny bit of blood with some protists in it to the next person it bites. This is how disease spreads.

Injections and pills can help to prevent protist diseases. Many harmful protists are found in dirty water. In some parts of the world, people do not have clean water, so they suffer from protist diseases.

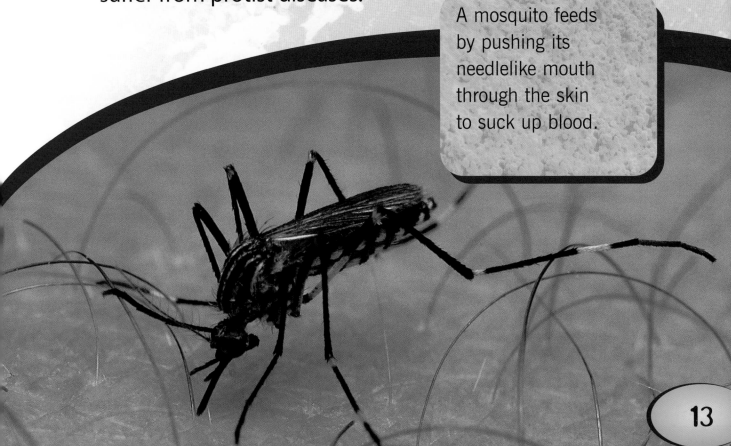

A mosquito feeds by pushing its needlelike mouth through the skin to suck up blood.

Some microlife is really rotten! It makes parts of a person's body go moldy, like old fruit. This is known as rotting or **decay**. It usually happens on the skin, or perhaps on a nail or inside the mouth. The tiny rotters that do this are called **fungi**. They are cousins of big fungi such as mushrooms and toadstools.

As microfungi grow in the skin, they make a tangle of tiny threads and blobs.

PET AND WASH
Some kinds of fungi can be caught from pets. It is important to wash your hands after handling a pet.

Fungi like damp skin, such as between the toes—so we should dry ourselves all over.

Itchy rashes

Some fungi can live on the skin. They make an itchy patch or rash, which can be red and sore. Problems caused by these fungi include **ringworm** and **athlete's foot**. If fungi affect the skin, a powder or cream from the pharmacist or doctor should kill them.

Keep Your Smile

Microlife can damage even the hardest parts of the body—the teeth. We need our teeth to bite and chew our food. So we must take great care of them. We need to brush them with toothpaste after meals, especially in the morning and last thing at night. Our teeth also need a regular check-up from the dentist.

BEWARE OF CANDY
Bacteria in the mouth love sweet, sugary foods. The more candy we eat, the more damage the bacteria can do to our teeth.

Tiny bacteria, shown here in blue, can cause holes and cracks in teeth.

This girl is at the dentist. He has shown her how to use a special pink pill to show where her teeth are dirty.

Yummy old food

Bits of old food get stuck on teeth. There are always some **bacteria** in the mouth, and they feed on the old food. As the bacteria feed, they make a substance called acid. This eats into the teeth and makes them soft or **decayed**. If the decay worsens, it causes toothache—which really hurts! We can fight this by brushing away the old food and bacteria.

Minibugs

Have you heard of nits? Nits look like specks of salt. They are usually stuck to hairs. It is difficult to get rid of them, even through normal washing and brushing. Nits are the eggs of head lice, which are tiny, blood-sucking insects. The bites from head lice cause itchy red patches on the skin.

Bedbugs bite!

Another small, blood-sucking insect is the bedbug. Bedbugs live in or under the bed, or in dusty corners. They creep out at night as people sleep, to suck their blood. Bedbug bites cause itchy red spots.

When we wash our clothes and bedding, we get rid of all kinds of minibugs and microlife.

Beating the minibugs

Special shampoos or creams get rid of lice and nits. Bedbugs can be killed by special powders or sprays. We also clean our homes, furniture, carpets, and beds, so the bugs do not come back.

This is a head louse. Lice hide among hairs or cling to skin with their hook-shaped legs.

HUGE MEAL

During one bite, a louse can suck in so much blood that its body gets five times bigger.

If a pet dog or cat scratches itself, it might be trying to get rid of fleas. A flea sucks blood, and its bites cause itchy spots. One kind of flea lives and feeds mainly on people. This human flea hides among our hairs. Human fleas carry germs that can cause diseases.

A flea has long, strong back legs, which help it to jump a long way.

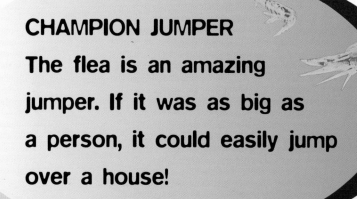

CHAMPION JUMPER

The flea is an amazing jumper. If it was as big as a person, it could easily jump over a house!

Animal fleas

Other kinds of fleas live mainly on pets such as cats and dogs. They also live on other animals such as raccoons, rats, and birds. These fleas may jump onto us and bite us. Then they jump off again and hide in carpets, furniture, cushions, curtains, and corners. If we keep our homes, ourselves and our pets clean, we can win the fight against fleas.

Pets scratch to get rid of fleas, but we can help with special flea collars, powders, or shampoos.

Itches and Wheezes

Mites and ticks are tiny cousins of spiders. Some of them bite people to suck their blood. They leave itchy spots or patches on the skin. The scabies mite burrows through the skin, causing terrible itching. Other kinds of mites and ticks live on animals such as sheep, deer, or pets. If they bite people, they can spread serious illnesses such as Lyme disease. This causes red skin patches, fever, and headache.

Lyme disease is spread when ticks that usually live on deer bite people instead.

HOME TO MILLIONS
An old mattress that is not cleaned properly might contain more than 1 million dust mites.

A mite has eight legs. This is the scabies mite, which causes horrible itching.

Dust mites

Some mites live in dust. They eat it, too. Like all creatures, dust mites produce droppings. When dust mite droppings become dry, they turn to powdery specks and float in the air. In some people, breathing in these specks can cause **asthma**, with wheezing and shortness of breath. To lessen the problem of asthma, we get rid of dust in our homes.

Earthworms wriggle in the soil. But some kinds of worms can wriggle in the body. Many live on the food in people's intestines (guts). Threadworms or pinworms are like tiny pieces of cotton thread. The roundworm grows as long as a pencil.

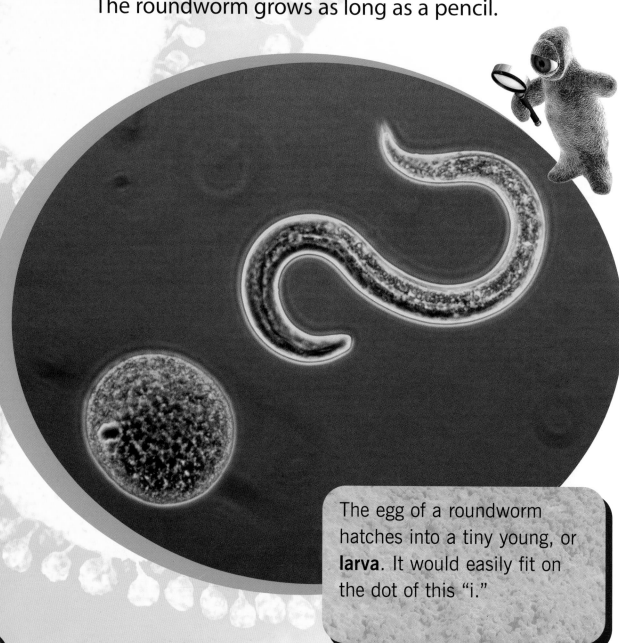

The egg of a roundworm hatches into a tiny young, or **larva**. It would easily fit on the dot of this "i."

Sneaky worms

Worms usually get into the body as tiny eggs, which are too small to see. The eggs might be on dirty hands, or in foods that have not been washed or cooked properly. We should wash our hands often, and make sure all foods are clean and fully cooked. The worms can be killed with special medicine.

In poor places, many people become ill because of worms. Health workers give out pills to kill the worms.

WORMS AND PETS

Tiny worms can come from the droppings of pets such as dogs and cats. They may get into people's eyes and damage eyesight. Pet droppings must be cleared up properly and we must wash our hands afterward.

Flukes and Suckers

The fluke is a small, leaf-shaped creature. It hatches from its tiny egg, gets into a snail, and grows. Next it leaves the snail and waits on a plant until it is eaten by a sheep or cow. Once inside, it grows more.

Sometimes the fluke then gets into a person— perhaps in sheep or cow meat that is not clean or cooked. Inside the body, the fluke feeds on the person's blood. Without medicine, the person could die.

round mouth

sucker

This leech is waving its mouth about as it searches for a meal of blood.

Lovely blood

Another small creature that loves blood is the leech.

It searches for big animals or people, and sucks their blood.

The leech sucks up so much blood that it swells up like a

red balloon. Lots of leeches on the body can make

a person very sick.

The leech has a
sucker at each end to
hold onto the skin.

MAKING ILLNESS WORSE

Long ago, doctors used to put
leeches onto people, to suck their
blood. The doctors thought this would
cure illness. But it often made
the people worse!

Every day, we battle against microlife. We keep ourselves, our clothes, and our homes clean. We wash our hands often, and make sure our food and water are safe and healthy. But there is a part of the battle that we cannot see. This happens inside our bodies.

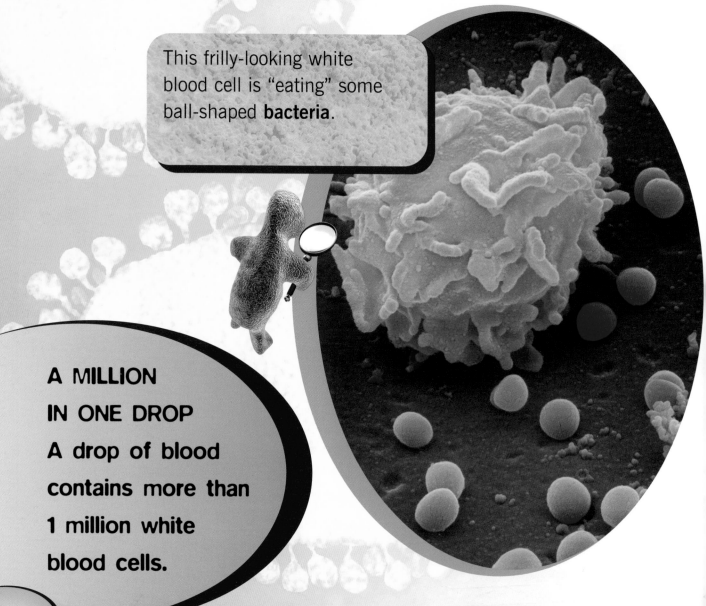

This frilly-looking white blood cell is "eating" some ball-shaped **bacteria**.

A MILLION IN ONE DROP
A drop of blood contains more than 1 million white blood cells.

Killing the germs

No matter how careful we are, a few germs always get into the body. Some of our best weapons against them are called white blood cells. There are different kinds of white blood cell. Some search for germs—and eat them! Others make substances called **antibodies**. The antibodies stick to germs and damage or destroy them. So our own bodies are always fighting against microlife that makes us sick.

Exercise, eating healthy foods, and keeping clean help our bodies to fight harmful microlife.

Find Out for Yourself

More Books to Read

Berger, Melvin, and Marilyn Hafner. *Germs Make Me Sick!* New York, N.Y.: HarperCollins, 1995.

Burnie, David. *Inside Guides: Microlife*. New York, N.Y.: Dorling Kindersley Family Library, 1997.

Frankel, Alona. *Prudence's Get Well Book*. New York, N.Y.: HarperCollins, 2000.

Royston, Angela. *Heinemann First Library: Tooth Decay*. Chicago, Ill.: Heinemann Library, 2004.

Using the Internet

Explore the Internet to find out more about microlife that makes us sick. Use a search engine and type in a keyword such as virus, vaccine, flea, or dust mite, or the name of a particular type of microlife.

Glossary

antibiotics medicine that kills germs called bacteria

antibody substance in the body that attacks and destroys germs

antiseptic substance that kills many kinds of germs. Antiseptics are safe to put on the skin.

asthma condition with many different causes, which makes breathing difficult and wheezy

athlete's foot itchy rash between the toes, caused by fungi

bacteria tiny living things. Some bacteria are helpful and some cause disease.

chickenpox illness with small, itchy red spots and patches on the skin

decay break apart and become rotten

disinfectant substance used for cleaning the home. Disinfectants kill many kinds of germs.

fungi group of living things including mushrooms, toadstools, and yeasts, which cause rotting

injection way of putting substances into the body using a sharp, hollow needle

larva young form of a small creature such as an insect, which hatches from an egg

malaria serious disease where the body gets very hot, trembles, and is very weak

measles illness with patches of itchy skin spots, sweating, and coughing

microscope equipment to make very small things look bigger

mumps illness where parts of the face swell and hurt

nutrients substances used by living things to grow and stay healthy

protist type of tiny living thing. Many protists look like specks of Jell-O.

ringworm illness where a fungus grows on the skin, forming a ring-shaped, itchy red patch

rubella (german measles) illness with small, flat, red patches on the skin

Streptococcus types of bacteria. Some types cause illnesses such as sore throats.

vaccination injection of a substance into the body, so it will not catch a certain disease in the future

virus smallest kind of living thing. All viruses cause illnesses, from common colds to deadly diseases.

Index